11/05

21.95

EVERYDAY SCIENCE

Under Pressure:

Forces

Ann Fullick

Heinemann
LIBRARY
Chicago, Illinois

© 2005 Heinemann Library
Published by Heinemann Library,
A division of Reed Elsevier, Inc.
Chicago, IL

For information, address the publisher:
Heinemann Library, 100 N. LaSalle, Suite 1200, Chicago, IL 60602
Customer Service: 888-363-4266
Visit our website at www.heinemannlibrary.com

Printed and bound in China by South China Printing Company.
08 07 06 05 04
10 9 8 7 6 5 4 3 2 1

Library of Congress Cataloging-in-Publication Data
Fullick, Ann, 1956-
  Under pressure : forces / Ann Fullick.
      p. cm. -- (Everyday science)
Summary: An overview of what forces are and how they affect the way we
live, describing such forces as gravity, pressure, balanced and
unbalanced forces, and motion on a curve.
Includes bibliographical references and index.
  ISBN 1-4034-4818-3 (HC), 1-4034-6424-3 (PB)
 1. Force and energy--Juvenile literature. [1. Force and energy.] I.
Title. II. Everyday science (Heinemann Library (Firm))
  QC73.4.F85 2004
  531'.6--dc22

                              2003014851

Acknowledgments
The publishers would like to thank the following for permission to reproduce photographs:
Action Plus pp.5, 24, 46; ARSTI/NASA p.30; CORBIS p.48; CORBIS/Franz-Marc Frei p.14; CORBIS/Gabe Palmer p.22; Getty 37; Harcourt Index pp. 4, 12, 25, 35; NASA pp. 31, 51; NOAA p.43; OSF/Keren Su p.41; OSF/Reed p.6; Photodisc pp. 36, 52; photolibrary.com p.45; Science Photo Library pp.28, 33; SPL/Colin Cuthbert p.21; SPL/Dr. Jeremy Burgess p.34; SPL/Geoff Tompkinson p.38; SPL/Hugh Turvey p.40; SPL/Jan Hinsch p.18; Sieve Tlyor p.11; Stockfile pp. 16, 47; The Car Photo Library p.9; Trip/D Sillitoe, Trip/C Wormald p.32; Trip/M Thornton p.26.

Cover photograph of a skateboarder reproduced by permission of Rex Features/Neale Haynes.

Artwork by Ascenders apart from Andrew Quelch p.23; Art Construction p.7; Jeremy Gower p.19; Mark Franklin pp. 27, 36.

The publishers would like to thank Robert Snedden for his assistance in the preparation of this book.

Every effort has been made to contact copyright holders of any material reproduced in this book. Any omissions will be rectified in subsequent printings if notice is given to the publishers.

Contents

Forces with You 4

Detecting and Measuring Forces 6
    Using Instruments 8
    Detecting Destructive Forces 10
    Measuring Natural Forces 12

Balanced and Unbalanced Forces 14

Speed and Acceleration 16

Stickability 18
    Using Friction 20
    Safety in Cars 22
    Moving in Water 24

Lifting and Levers 26

Gravity 28
    Gravity Everywhere 30
    The Turning Tides 32
    Plants and Gravity 34
    Overcoming Gravity 36

Pressure 38
    Watch Your Feet! 40
    Air Pressure 42
    Forces in Fluids 44

Motion in a Curve 46
    Forces and Fun 48

Forces into the Future 50

Summary: Forces All Around Us 52

Glossary 53

Further Reading 55

Index 56

Forces with You

You have just settled down for a good read, but here are a few things to try out first. Jump up in the air. Drop your book—carefully! Walk across the room. Open the door. Stand still on Earth's surface without floating away into space. If you have managed to do all of these things, you are already expert at using forces.

What are forces?

Forces are pushes or pulls that can change the shape of an object or its movement. They are invisible—but we know they are there because of their effects. Although we cannot see forces, we can measure them. The unit of force is the newton (N), named after Sir Isaac Newton, a famous English scientist whose work on forces changed the way people thought about the world.

Forces everywhere

Forces—the pushes and pulls that make things happen—are a key part of everyday life. Without the force of gravity we would float away into space. There also would be no life on Earth because its atmosphere would float away, too. Our cars depend on forces to get them moving, to slow them down, and to change direction. We do not have to travel in a car to need forces. They are important whenever you move, and the human body has some amazing adaptations that allow it to deal with the forces it meets every day.

Reaching high
Forces on a spectacular scale pushed mountains like these thousands of yards or meters into the sky.

Natural forces, artificial power

Forces are responsible for the very shape of the world around us. Earth is round as a result of gravitational forces. The mountains that shape our landscapes came about because of powerful forces under Earth's surface pushing together. Many great valleys have been formed over millions of years by the forces exerted by water flowing over them.

Forces in the natural world can be huge, but forces also work on a very small scale. For example, our ability to hear each other speak depends on forces, tiny pushes that move the working parts of our ears, enabling us to pick up and respond to the sounds all around us.

For thousands of years, people have recognized the importance of forces. Even if they have not always fully understood them, they have certainly known how to use them. Fantastic monuments like the pyramids in Egypt, the statues on Easter Island, and Stonehenge in England were built because our ancestors had developed an understanding of how to use forces to make work easier. That process of using forces to make life easier continues today. You can see it in action around you in everything from a can opener to a scooter, from the family car to a pair of scissors. We have developed giant machines to produce forces for us, forces that have enabled us to take over almost every corner of the world, and a tiny piece of space as well.

Detecting and Measuring Forces

Forces are pushes and pulls. We can detect them and measure them, but only indirectly. What we sense or measure is the effect of a force—the change in movement or shape that it causes—not the force itself. We have natural force detectors in our own bodies, and we have developed a range of instruments for measuring all kinds of forces.

Sensing forces
Animals' whiskers are sensitive to forces.

How sensitive are you?

Your sense of touch is vital for letting you know which part of you is in contact with someone or something else, whether you are holding something soft or sharp. This sensitivity depends on your skin, a huge organ for sensing forces. Your skin covers about 22 square feet (2 m^2), and contains millions of nerve endings—over 4,000,000 for responding to a light touch, plus thousands more for heavy pressure!

Which way up are you? What position is your body in now? What sounds can you hear around you? Are you moving or not? You can answer these questions because your body is sensitive to forces in the world around you. What is more, the animals and plants that share our everyday lives also have their own force sensors.

Forces in the ear

Sound is made up of pressure waves traveling through the air. We pick up the pressure changes through the delicate mechanism of our ears. The pinna, on the outside, collects the sounds. The eardrum is pushed in by the pressure of the sound waves. The eardrum, in turn, pushes against the small bones in the middle ear, which then push on another membrane. When the pressure in the wave decreases, the eardrum moves out again. This back-and-forth motion sets up more pressure waves in the fluid in the inner ear. These are detected by sensitive cells that send impulses off to the brain.

Hearing is not the only force detection that goes on in the ear. The semicircular canals are sense organs in their own right. They give us information about the position of our head. For this reason, they are very important to us in keeping our balance. The fluid inside the semicircular canals moves in response to forces as we tilt or move our heads, affecting sensitive hair cells. The hair cells send information to our brain, where it is interpreted to give us a sense of our position in space.

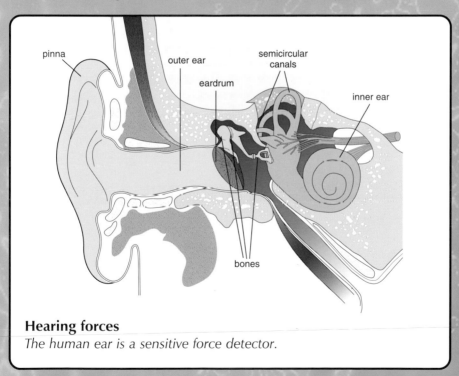

Hearing forces
The human ear is a sensitive force detector.

Human beings are sensitive to forces. This makes it much easier for us to manage our everyday lives successfully. Even in the 21st century, sensitivity to forces is very important to human survival!

Using Instruments

It is great having bodies that are sensitive to different forces, but it is also important to be able to measure forces outside our bodies. Because we cannot measure forces directly, our instruments measure the effect the forces have on things.

The basic instrument for measuring simple forces is the newtonmeter. Some newtonmeters are better at measuring pulls, others at measuring pushes. Almost everyone has at least one newtonmeter in their home, although we usually call them by a much simpler name—scales!

Measuring weight

Everything is made up of a certain amount of material (stuff). This is its mass, and it stays the same wherever the object is, even in outer space. But the force anything exerts on Earth's surface is affected not just by its mass but also by the pull of gravity. (We'll be looking at gravity in more detail later in this book.) So when you lift something off the ground, you have to overcome the pull of gravity on its mass. This force is called weight. Weight is a widely measured force in everyday life—we watch our weight, we buy food by weight, elevators have weight limits. Because weight is a force, it should be measured in newtons. Your weight in newtons is approximately equal to your mass in kilograms multiplied by ten.

This is where things get tricky. Although a scale actually measures our weight, it is designed to show our mass in pounds or kilograms. In science, we have to take great care to use the words *mass* and *weight* correctly, which can be difficult because in everyday life we tend to use them incorrectly. For example, in everyday terms we would say a bag of sugar weighs 2.2 pounds, or 1 kilogram. However, if we were talking scientifically, and correctly, we would say that the bag of sugar has a mass of 2.2 pounds, or 1 kilogram, and its weight on Earth is 10 newtons. In this book we are looking at the science in everyday situations, so we must take extra care not to get confused.

Measuring forces in a car

As we shall see, forces are responsible for changing movement. Nothing moves at all unless a force acts upon it. Then once something is moving, it will continue in a straight line unless another force acts upon it. So when we start our car moving and drive around in it, we are using several forces.

Use with care
Big forces are involved in moving and stopping a car. We use very powerful engines and brakes to produce these forces.

Both speed and direction are important when we travel in a car. However, we do not usually measure the exact forces that are being applied at any point as we drive along. Instead, we measure the overall effect of those forces. So the speedometer measures speed and shows changes in speed. In other words, when forces make a car accelerate, what is measured is how the speed of the car changes over time.

Detecting Destructive Forces

Forces make things move and change direction—but they can also be used to make things change shape. Imagine yourself in the kitchen, with a ball of pastry and a rolling pin. By applying force to the rolling pin, you can change the shape of the ball of pastry. By squeezing and stretching the pastry, you could reform it completely. This is a simple example of the way forces can be used to make things change their shape.

Often these changes are exactly what we want. But if you apply too much force, the pastry turns out too thin, so it tears. If you apply too little force, the pastry will be too thick. In the same way, when forces are used in industry, the right amount of force must be used for the desired effect. For example, the sheet metal used in car bodies has to be just the right thickness to combine lightness, cheapness, and strength. So it is important to have an effective way to measure the force (pressure) of the rollers that produce the sheets.

Taking the strain!

Sometimes forces acting in one way—making a car move or holding up the weight of a bridge—can have other, unwanted effects. Forces can bend metals and plastics out of shape, and these shape changes can be dangerous. The materials can be weakened and eventually snap, with potentially catastrophic results. So we use instruments to keep track of how materials are affected by the forces acting on them and to give us warning of any problems.

Strain gauges are used to detect potentially dangerous stresses in materials. They are also used to weigh very large objects. A stress is a force that can change the shape of an object, while a strain is the change in shape that happens as a result of the stress. Think of the huge trucks you see delivering goods all around the country. They travel thousands of miles over roads and bridges, and also across the ocean to other countries. For many reasons—safety, cost of ferry crossings, payment for transportation—people need to know exactly how much these huge vehicles weigh. Semi trucks have their own weighbridges. The wheels are positioned over strain gauges to figure out the force involved and the weight of the whole vehicle.

How do strain gauges work?

In many cases a strain gauge is made up of a wire, or wires, that carry a small electric current. When the strain gauge is affected by a stress—compressed or stretched, for example—the wire is affected and its resistance to the electric current is changed so that more or less electricity flows. This change in the current is picked up by sensors and interpreted in terms of a particular stress.

Some strain gauges are designed to measure compression when an object is squeezed. Others are designed to measure a change in shape when an object is stretched. They can help us measure a wide range of forces and their effects.

Heavyweight vehicles

The forces that the largest vehicles exert on our road surfaces and bridges are huge. Some of the biggest semi trucks have a mass of around 71 tons (65 metric tons)—so their weight is 650,000 newtons. No wonder roads always seem to need maintenance work! Many of them were not built with such loads in mind.

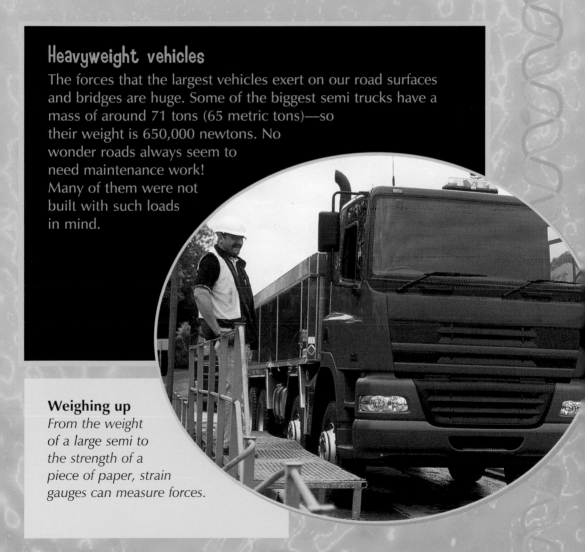

Weighing up
From the weight of a large semi to the strength of a piece of paper, strain gauges can measure forces.

Measuring Natural Forces

Walk up to a tree and try to push it over. Then try to lift your family car. Exert as much force as you can, but the tree is probably still standing, and the car is still firmly on the ground. Generating forces this big is beyond most of us. Yet wind, water, and Earth's moving continents can do these things easily. The forces that can be generated in the natural world are almost unimaginably powerful.

Wind power

We have all experienced a windy day and seen how easily small things are carried away. Many of us have experienced a severe gale, when trees are uprooted and roofs blow off. Hurricanes and tornadoes can flatten whole areas and carry houses, cars, and animals far through the air. Wind speed is measured using an anemometer, an instrument with cups that are pushed around by the wind. The speed of their rotation is measured and converted into a measurement of the wind speed. The faster the wind, the stronger it is and the greater the forces it can exert.

Tough and flexible
Bridges like this have to have some give, or flexibility, to let them safely absorb the force of high wind.

Earth moves

The ground beneath your feet and the scenery around you have all been formed by the most powerful forces known to us—the movements of Earth's surface itself. Earth's crust is a thin, solid layer of rock floating on a mantle of incredibly hot semiliquid rock below. This crust is cracked into a number of large pieces called tectonic plates. The tectonic plates move at a rate of a little more than an inch, or a few centimeters, each year. If two plates that are sliding past each other get stuck for some reason, huge forces build up until the rocks are suddenly released, moving several yards or meters in a fraction of a second and causing an earthquake.

Measuring earthquakes

Earthquake strength is measured using the Richter scale, which usually ranges from 1 to 9. Each number represents a tenfold increase in strength. So an earthquake rated as 5 is ten times more powerful than one rated as 4. An earthquake measuring 1 on the scale is detected only by seismographs—we don't feel it. At 7 we have a major earthquake, causing heavy damage and possible loss of life.

Almost everyone is familiar with television images showing the destruction these displays of raw force can bring. In the Los Angeles earthquake of 1994, 57 people died and thousands of buildings were destroyed. The earthquake measured 6.7 on the Richter scale. In areas that are less prepared for an earthquake's devastating effects, the destruction and loss of life are even greater. The earthquake that shook the ancient Iranian city of Bam in 2003 also measured 6.7 on the Richter scale, but it killed an estimated 30,000 people, injured approximately the same number, and left about 80,000 people homeless.

The science of prediction

Measuring these huge forces at work is an important part of predicting when and where earthquakes are likely to happen. They use instruments called seismographs. Seismographs pick up any Earth movement and record it. If the ground is still, a seismograph records a straight line. The greater the forces moving the ground, the more wiggly the line that is produced.

Balanced and Unbalanced Forces

Imagine two teams lined up for a tug of war, with the rope lying on the ground in position. The rope does not move forward or backward because nobody is pulling on it. Imagine that the teams pick up the rope, take up the slack, and start to pull. But the marker on the rope remains exactly over the center point. This time the lack of movement certainly is not because no one is pulling on the rope. One glance at the straining muscles and red faces of our imaginary teams will show that very strong pulling forces are being exerted on it. The point is, the pulls in each direction are the same. The forces are balanced, and so no change in movement results.

Now imagine that one team starts to tire. They cannot pull as hard, and slowly the other team heaves the marker toward themselves and finally over their own line. They have won because they exerted a larger force than the losing team. As a result, the forces became unbalanced and so the rope's movement changed. When forces are unbalanced, things move.

Balanced forces

What happens when forces act depends on their balance. Many things in life stay the same—a book sits on your desk, you sit still on the chair, and your clothes stay on the bedroom floor! It is not that no forces act on the objects, but that the forces in different directions are balanced, just as at the start of the tug of war. The weight of the book pushing down on your desk is balanced by the force of the desk pushing up on your book (yes, that is really what happens). The weight of you pushing down on the chair is balanced by the chair pushing up on you. The forces are balanced, and so nothing moves.

Forces can be balanced even when things are moving. When a car travels along the road at a steady speed, the forces that are causing it to speed up are balanced out by the forces that are slowing it down. So the speed stays the same. When forces are balanced, things stay the same.

Unbalanced forces

Hold out your hand with a book on it. The forces are balanced, with the weight of the book pushing downward and your hand providing an equal and opposite upward force. Now pull your hand away from the book—what happens? The forces are no longer balanced. Gravity is still pulling the book downward but there is no upward force to oppose it. As a result, the book drops to the floor, where the forces become balanced again.

Unbalanced forces affect the way things move. Unbalanced forces start something moving, and the object will move in the direction of the force applied to it—the book falls straight downward. If something is already moving when an unbalanced force is applied to it, it may speed up, slow down, or change direction, depending on the direction of the unbalanced force.

Pulling together
A tug of war is a great example of the difference between balanced and unbalanced forces.

Speed and Acceleration

Riding a bike is a great way of getting from one place to another. What forces are acting on you as you ride along? Moving things are affected by two opposing sets of forces—the forces pushing it forward and the forces pulling it back. For movement to start, the forward forces (thrust) must be greater than the forces slowing it down (drag).

What a drag

On a bike the thrust is provided by your legs as you pedal forward. The drag is produced by a very important force—friction. Frictional forces are caused by surfaces sticking together as they move past each other. When you are cycling along, the air rushing past you and your bike creates friction. All the time you are accelerating, these forces are unbalanced, with your legs producing the larger force—thrust.

Battling forces
Cycling involves a constant battle between the thrust your legs can produce and the forces that drag you backward.

Fantastic speeds

The fastest people in the world on bikes are all men. This is because they have a bigger proportion of muscle in their legs than women and so can produce a bigger thrust. Their times are amazing:

- 200 meters   Curtis Hamett   9.865 seconds
- 1,000 meters   Arnaud Tournant   58.875 seconds
- 4,000 meters   Chris Boardman   4 minutes 11.114 seconds

Once you are cycling along at a steady speed, the thrust and drag forces are balanced. The change comes when you want to slow down and stop. If you do not mind taking your time to slow down, you can do so by just stopping pedaling. This happens because only drag forces are acting, so you will come to a stop. Usually we want to stop more quickly, though, so we use the brakes. Bike brakes work by increasing the frictional forces acting on the wheels, making it much harder to push them around. By stopping pedaling and squeezing the brakes, you greatly increase the force acting backwards on you and your bike. As a result your bike stops very quickly.

What affects acceleration?

When we move, and particularly when we race, acceleration is important. So what affects our rate of acceleration? Again, it all comes down to forces—the size of the thrust, the size of the drag, and the mass of the object being moved. The acceleration and speed you can go on your bike will be very different from the speed of professional racing cyclists. Speed cyclists try hard to make themselves as aerodynamic as possible, so the forward forces are as large, and the backward forces are as small, as possible. Professional cyclists also have very strong legs, so they can produce a much bigger thrust. Their clothing, bikes, and tires are designed to reduce the frictional forces as much as possible. Finally, the mass of the object being moved is important. Their bikes are built of light, strong materials. You will have seen this effect in reverse if you have ever tried to ride your bike with a passenger or while carrying heavy bags. Extra mass makes it much harder to accelerate because you need so much more thrust.

Stickability

Imagine going out on a really cold, frosty morning, finding a frozen puddle, and sliding on it. Your feet slip easily on the smooth surface, but if you try to walk normally it is not so easy. Now imagine the same place on a dry morning and the situation will be reversed—you can walk fine, but any attempt at sliding is likely to end in a fall. The difference has to do with friction.

Not so smooth
Surfaces that look smooth are actually rough, as this highly magnified picture of a polished metal surface shows.

Slowing down

Frictional forces slow down moving objects. The force always acts in the direction opposite of the direction in which the object is moving. Frictional forces are the result either of solid surfaces rubbing together as movement occurs, or of the resistance of water or air to things passing through them. The rougher the solid surfaces are, the more friction there is when they rub against each other.

As the surfaces rub against each other, they give off heat—try rubbing your hands together hard to feel the heating effects of friction. One of the clearest examples of the effect of friction is the difference between cycling on a road, on grass, or in sand or mud. The more friction there is between the two surfaces, the stronger the force slowing down the forward movement. Anyone who has tried to cycle along a beach knows that sand is by far the most difficult surface to cycle on.

Overcoming friction

Sometimes frictional forces are a nuisance. They slow things down or stop them when we do not want them to. However, we have developed ways of overcoming friction and keeping things running smoothly. Here is one of them.

Car engines produce the forward thrust that allows us to drive around. However, in the engine many metal parts rub together. Although the metal is highly polished and smooth, this causes friction. Friction would make the metal parts get hot, expand, and stick together. The engine might even explode!

The friction problems in an engine are overcome by using oil. The oil acts as a lubricant, keeping the two surfaces slightly apart so they glide smoothly past each other. Various types and thicknesses of oil are used to lubricate a wide range of machinery. At home we lubricate door locks, sewing machines, and bicycle chains, for example. In industry, without lubrication the big machines would grind to a halt.

Lubricating the joints

Swing your arm around from the shoulder—if bone were grating on bone inside your joint, friction would mean the joint would wear out. Fortunately, our joints have two defenses:
- The ends of the bones are covered in a smooth, slippery substance called cartilage that protects the bone and reduces friction.
- Between the ends of the bones, a liquid called synovial fluid is produced. This lubricates the joint and prevents the bones from rubbing together.

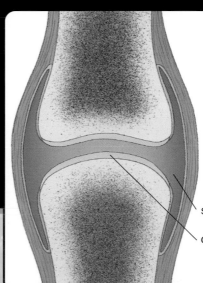

Smoothing you out
Your knee is constantly moving and flexing, but cartilage and synovial fluid help avoid damage caused by friction.

synovial fluid

cartilage

Using Friction

There are times when frictional forces are really useful to us.

Friction for stopping

The brakes on your bike use friction to slow you down. The rubber pads press on the rim of the wheel, create friction, and slow the wheel. By stopping pedaling and then braking, you stop the forward thrust and increase the amount of friction, so the bike stops quickly. The brakes on motor vehicles work on a similar principle. It takes a lot of frictional force to slow a car traveling at 50 miles (80 km) per hour, and the brake pads get very hot when they are applied. Some of their material is worn away every time you brake, so it is important to check brakes regularly and replace them if they are worn.

Stopping takes time

When a car is traveling at 20 or 30 miles (32 or 48 km) per hour, it takes less braking force to stop it than if it is traveling at 60 or 70 miles (96 or 112 km) per hour. With the same braking force, a vehicle will take longer to stop when traveling fast than when traveling slowly. It will therefore also travel farther before it stops. Drivers must leave enough stopping distance between their car and the car in front. This distance depends on speed, and so it will change during a trip. Many traffic accidents are caused by people traveling too close to the car in front. If that vehicle stops suddenly, the car behind cannot stop before the vehicles collide.

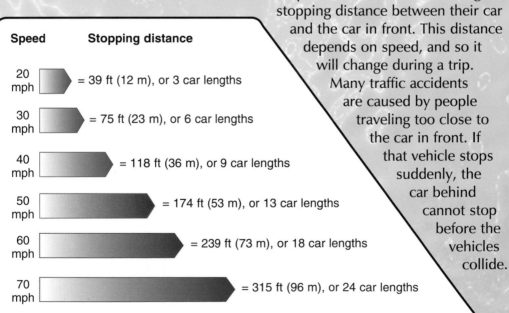

Speed	Stopping distance
20 mph	= 39 ft (12 m), or 3 car lengths
30 mph	= 75 ft (23 m), or 6 car lengths
40 mph	= 118 ft (36 m), or 9 car lengths
50 mph	= 174 ft (53 m), or 13 car lengths
60 mph	= 239 ft (73 m), or 18 car lengths
70 mph	= 315 ft (96 m), or 24 car lengths

Using force
If all drivers understood force and remembered to leave these correct stopping distances, there would be fewer traffic accidents.

Making tracks

Tire treads are important for maintaining contact with the road. This creates the frictional forces needed for cars to brake effectively.

Talking tires

Whether on a bike or in a car, your tires have a major effect on how safe you are. Tires are the point of contact between your vehicle and the road. The more friction there is between your tires and the road, the less likely you are to skid.

Safe air

In 1888 John Dunlop, an Irish veterinary surgeon, patented the first inflatable, or pneumatic, rubber tires.

Inflatable tires are far safer than the solid rubber tires that had been used previously because, under pressure, much more of the tire surface makes contact with the road, increasing the stabilizing effect of friction.

On a dry, smooth road surface with no oil on it, the ideal tires would be fairly wide and completely smooth—just like the slicks used by Formula 1 cars in dry weather. There are several problems with smooth tires for ordinary cars or bikes, however. First, completely smooth roads with no oil or grease on them are not very common. Second, in most places it rains sometimes. Water on the road acts as a lubricant. So smooth tires would slide over the surface, losing almost all of their frictional forces and putting the car or bike into a skid. To make sure they work in both wet and dry conditions, tires have grooves, or treads. Treads increase the frictional forces if the road surface is wet. The grooves help to push water out of the way of the raised areas of the tire, keeping it in contact with the road and making braking effective.

Safety in Cars

You probably have seen cars presented as exciting, attractive, speedy, and desirable. Ask people what they want in a family car and they will probably look for safety and economy as well as looks and speed. Car designers need a very thorough understanding of the relationships between forces and motion to be able to make cars as fast, attractive, safe, and economical as possible.

Good looks and good performance

For a car to go fast, the frictional (drag) forces between the car and the air must be as small as possible. Cars with small drag forces are more economical, too, because less fuel is needed to produce the thrust needed to overcome drag. So a streamlined shape that moves easily though the air is an important design feature.

Dealing with collisions

Traveling in cars may well be the most dangerous thing we do. Accidents can happen, sometimes as a result of our own carelessness, sometimes because of other drivers. For car designers, this is the key point. They have to try to ensure that in a collision the people inside the car will be unharmed.

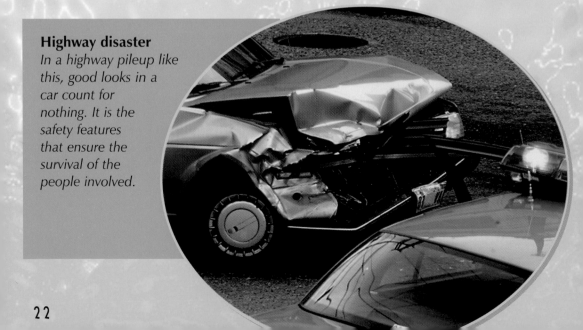

Highway disaster
In a highway pileup like this, good looks in a car count for nothing. It is the safety features that ensure the survival of the people involved.

Safety features in cars

Crumple zones

In a collision, crumple zones crumple to absorb the huge energy exerted at impact. They also help prevent damage to the part of the car where you sit.

Impact-absorbing bumpers

If you hit something while moving slowly, the bumpers absorb the force of the impact.

Airbags

Many cars now have airbags that inflate almost instantaneously in a collision. Your body squashes the airbag, which spreads the forces involved over a much wider area and also slows down the rate at which your body stops moving.

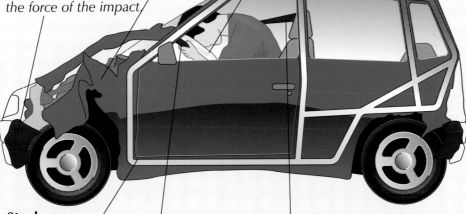

Steel cage

It takes a huge amount of force to deform this rigid steel cage, so it will protect you in a crash.

Padding and collapsing steering wheels

In a crash, your head or body may hit the inside of the car. Padding and collapsible steering wheels help absorb some forces so that your body is affected as little as possible.

Seat belts

If your car stops suddenly, you will keep moving forward until you hit something, probably something hard, such as the dashboard or the windshield. This will slow you down very quickly. Your body will experience an enormous force that might injure or even kill you. Seat belts help stop this from happening. They stretch slightly as they stop you, so your body is subjected to a much smaller force—and you are much less likely to be seriously injured.

Moving in Water

When you walk down the street, forces act on you. One of those forces is the frictional force of air resistance. You have to use energy to move your body through the air, though you do not usually notice it. If you are running, or it is a windy day, you might notice the air resistance. But it is a very different story when you try to move in water.

Water resistance

Imagine wading at the edge of a lake of the ocean—the water forms splashes and ripples as you move your feet along. Then imagine moving farther out—up to your waist—and walking along again. It would soon become tiring because water is much thicker than air, and so the frictional forces on your body are much greater. The drag would be so great that your legs would begin to ache and you would soon want to get out of the water. Water resistance makes running in the water even more difficult.

Seriously streamlined
Competitive swimmers wear smooth caps and full body suits of special material to reduce drag.

Overcoming water resistance

Moving forward, as we have seen, is the result of unbalanced forces in which the forward force is bigger than the frictional forces. Because of water resistance, it is hard for a person to move through water in the same way as he or she moves on land. To move easily through water, we have developed different methods of moving. The most obvious way is swimming. When you swim, you make your body shape streamlined. This reduces water resistance as much as possible, so you can move more easily.

Shark shape
The streamlined body shape of sharks has changed little over millions of years. Their body shape makes them the ultimate swimming machine.

We are not the only animals to move easily through water. Most of us have seen fish swimming around in a tank, a pond, a stream, or an aquarium. Fish are beautifully streamlined and can move through the water with ease, usually far faster than any human swimmer.

Building boats

Just as car designers have to understand forces before they can develop safe, fast cars, so boat designers have to understand the forces that act on boats. One important factor is water resistance. So for a boat to move through the water as quickly as possible, the hull must be streamlined.

Fishy birds

Penguins are comically awkward-looking to the human eye. Their bodies are compact, and their legs are very short. They are poorly adapted for moving fast over land. As for flying—forget it! Their wings look more like fins and cannot lift them into the air. But in the water, they are graceful, fast, and beautiful. That is what they are designed for—to swim effectively.

Lifting and Levers

Remember what it feels like to play on a seesaw, going up and down, bouncing your playmate up into the air. Remember, too, how frustrating it was if the two people on the seesaw both weighed the same, and there was no grown-up around to get you started.

Getting moving

The seesaw reminds us of the difference between balanced and unbalanced forces. When forces are balanced, nothing happens. If the two children are of equal mass and they sit the same distance from the middle of the seesaw, the seesaw will be balanced and will not move unless another force is applied—for example, a downward push on one end by an adult. Once the movement is started, the children can supply a push (force) with their feet when they touch the ground and keep the seesaw moving.

Balancing act
Seesaws are fun only if you get the forces right.

Using levers

If two people who weigh about the same are using a seesaw, they both sit at the ends. However, you can still use a seesaw even if one person is much heavier than the other—an adult and a child, for example. The overall downward force is a result of both the mass of the person and the distance they are sitting from the moving point—the fulcrum, or pivot—of the seesaw. So if the child sits at the end of the seesaw, and the adult sits closer to the fulcrum, the downward forces will balance out and they can use the seesaw easily. This is the principle of a lever.

A lever is a useful tool for lifting something heavy. The heavy object is attached to one end of the lever, close to the fulcrum. A force is then applied to the other end of the lever a long way from the pivot. Even a fairly small force applied to a long lever can lift a very heavy object.

There are many different types of levers, depending on how the fulcrum, the load, and the effort are arranged. But they all help us lift heavy masses more easily and smoothly than we could without them. The wheelbarrow you use in the yard is one example of a lever. The fulcrum is in the middle of the wheel, the load is close to the fulcrum, and your hands are as far away as possible. The huge cranes used in building construction are also examples of levers used to lift huge loads. There is another lever that you use every day—your elbow joint! The load is on your hand, the fulcrum is at the elbow itself and the lifting force is supplied by the muscles that attach the bones of your forearm to your upper arm.

Why levers?

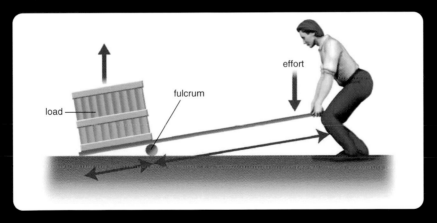

Let's calculate the mechanical advantage (MA) levers provide.

$$\text{mechanical advantage} = \frac{\text{length of lever's effort arm}}{\text{length of lever's load arm}}$$

- effort arm = distance from fulcrum to lifting force
- load arm = distance from load to fulcrum

So using a crowbar, you can in theory lift something eight times heavier than you could alone. In practice you will have to waste some effort overcoming friction.

Gravity

Everything, if allowed to, falls toward the ground because of one of the best-known forces in the universe—gravity.

Essential gravity

Gravity is a force associated with all bodies. It pulls everything toward the center of that body. The most important example in our everyday lives is Earth's gravitational force, which pulls us all down toward the center. Without gravity, we would all go floating off Earth's surface. The atmosphere that provides us with oxygen would float away, too. We need gravity.

Earth's gravity was involved in the shaping of Earth. We only started to understand gravity about 300 years ago. We owe our understanding to a scientist named Isaac Newton and (so the story goes) an apple!

Sir Isaac Newton

Isaac Newton was born on December 25, 1642, in Lincolnshire, England. His father had died, and Isaac was born early. He was so small and weak that the doctor warned his mother that he would probably die. He lived, and his grandmother raised him after his mother remarried. He did poorly in school. He was more interested in math, which was not taught, than in Latin and Greek. At sixteen he left formal education and tried without success to run the family farm. He spent his time reading and working on math and science problems, while his sheep escaped and damaged his neighbor's crops. Newton even ended up in court!

Isaac Newton
Newton was a lonely, rather unpleasant man with few friends. But he was one of the greatest scientific geniuses of all time.

Eventually Newton's uncle and old schoolteacher talked his mother into letting him go to Cambridge University. There he thrived. In 1665 the university was closed down temporarily to prevent the spread of the terrible disease called plague, and Newton continued his studies at home. During this time he invented mathematical calculus, did experiments in which he showed that white light is made up of many colors, and made his famous discoveries about gravity.

The apple story

The story says that Newton was sitting in the orchard when an apple fell on his head. He wondered why the apple fell down rather than up or sideways. These thoughts led him to his theory of gravity. Evidence suggests this story is at least based in fact. Newton often went out into the orchard to think about tricky problems, and at this point he was trying to determine why the Moon goes around Earth. An apple falling—though probably not onto his head—gave him the idea of a force pulling downward. He linked that thought to children whirling objects such as balls around their heads on a rope. They seemed like models of the Moon circling Earth. Putting the two ideas together gave Newton a model of the Moon traveling around Earth, held in place by a downward force (gravity)—the same force that caused the apple to fall in the orchard. Newton's simple idea would be the basis of physical science from then, right through the 21st century.

Gravity Everywhere

Isaac Newton developed his laws of gravitation (or gravitas, as he called it) in 1665. But it was over twenty years before he shared his information with everyone else by publishing it in a book. By then, he had figured out many details and some very complex mathematical formulas about it—all of which are still used today.

Everything has gravity

One of Newton's ideas was that everything has its own gravity. It is a strange thought that every object exerts a gravitational pull on every other object, but it is true. The size of the gravitational force is directly proportional to the mass of the object. The only reason that you do not have pencils, erasers, bits of food, and other people constantly attracted to you is because you simply are not big enough. Your gravitational pull is very, very small. It is only when an object is as big and massive as a moon, planet, or star that we notice the effects of its gravity.

Different sizes, different gravity

Now we know that the gravitational pull of an object is linked to its mass, we can understand why the gravity on the Moon is so much less than the gravity here on Earth (only about a sixth as strong). It is because the Moon is much smaller and less massive than Earth. This smaller gravitational force is the reason why we would weigh less on the Moon than we do here on Earth, and why the astronauts who visited the Moon in the 1960s and 1970s could move about so easily, even in their bulky spacesuits.

Walking on the Moon
Very few people have traveled in space. But most of us have seen pictures of astronauts walking on the surface of the Moon.

Earth and Moon

Earth exerts a gravitational force on the Moon. And the Moon exerts one back on Earth. Earth's gravity keeps the Moon in orbit, but how does it work? Keeping one object in orbit around another involves unbalanced forces. Otherwise the orbiting object would simply travel away in a straight line. When an object orbits Earth, the force pulling it toward Earth (gravity) is set against its forward velocity, so that the Moon (or other orbiting body) is always falling toward Earth but never gets there.

To help explain this, imagine whirling a ball around your head on a string. The ball has forward motion, but the string keeps it moving in a circle around you by exerting a force on the ball that acts toward you. If you replace yourself with Earth and the ball with the Moon, gravity is the equivalent of the string joining you to the ball.

Swinging around

The Moon stays in orbit around Earth because of unbalanced gravitational forces. These forces mean that the Moon is always pulled toward Earth but never falls onto it.

The Turning Tides

When the tide is out, it is a long walk to the sea, but if the tide comes in sooner than you expect, your towels get soaked. Gravity is at work. The tidal movements of the ocean are largely caused by the gravitational pull of the Moon. As the Moon circles Earth, its gravity pulls the sea toward it. This produces a high tide. Once it has passed, the sea falls back again to make a low tide. This happens twice a day in most places.

St. Michael's Mount, Cornwall, England
At high tide the Mount is cut off from the mainland. At low tide you can walk across to it. This change in water level is caused by the gravitational pull of the Moon.

Sun and tide

The Sun's gravitational pull also has a weak effect on our tides. At new Moon and full Moon, it works with the Moon to give the exceptionally high spring tides. At the first and third quarters, it works against the Moon to cause neap tides, which are relatively low high tides.

Gravity and you

Gravity is important to all living things on Earth because it keeps us in place. But gravity has other effects on our bodies that are harder to notice. Our muscles constantly work against gravity to keep us upright and stable. The human body is not a simple shape like a ball or a cube, and we change position all the time. Every time we stick a part of our body out of line, the gravitational forces acting on us change. To keep us from falling over, our muscles are constantly making tiny adjustments. We realize how effective they are only when we faint and find ourselves slumped on the floor.

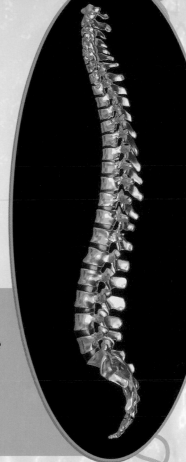

Gravity shields
The cartilage discs between the vertebrae of the spine can be clearly seen as blue discs in this computer illustration.

These constant movements against gravity are the reason why it is so tiring being a car passenger on a long trip. The movement of the car as it speeds up, slows down, and turns constantly shifts your body and changes the forces acting to pull it down. Hundreds of posture muscles have to work to keep you upright, and so you feel tired at the end of the trip. Passengers can feel more tired than the driver. This is because the driver knows when changes in speed and direction are coming and is supported by the steering wheel.

Incredible shrinking you

If you measure your height first thing in the morning and again just before bed, you will notice a difference. Most people are tallest the first thing in the morning and shrink by up to a half inch (1 cm) during the day. This is a result of Earth's gravity. Between the small bones called vertebrae that make up your spine there are pads of rubbery tissue called cartilage. Cartilage acts as a shock absorber, cushioning the bones as you move around and jar them. But all day the force of gravity pulls down on your body, and the weight crushes these cartilage discs. By the end of the day, each one is slightly compressed, and the overall shrinkage can be measured. When you lie in bed, gravity is no longer compressing your spine, so the cartilage recovers. In the morning you have gained height again.

Plants and Gravity

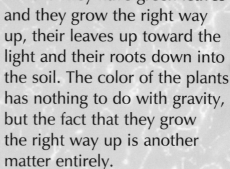

Think about some plants. They could be trees in a forest, crops in a field, flowering plants in a garden, or house plants in a pot. They all have certain things in common. They have green leaves and they grow the right way up, their leaves up toward the light and their roots down into the soil. The color of the plants has nothing to do with gravity, but the fact that they grow the right way up is another matter entirely.

Dancing plants

Scientists are not sure how plants manage their geotropisms (responses to gravity). Some seem to have clusters of starch granules, called statoliths, in some of their cells. These statoliths are heavy and fall to the bottom of root and shoot cells in response to gravity. They then appear to affect the way the cells grow, so the plant part grows either toward or away from the direction of gravity.

Growing up

When a seed starts to grow below the surface of the soil, it is in the dark. But there is only a limited supply of food in the seed. For this reason, it is important that the new shoot grows up into the light so that the leaves can open and make food. At the same time, the new roots must grow downward to anchor the tiny plant and take up water and minerals from the soil. Plants manage this because they are sensitive to the force of gravity. The roots grow in the same direction as the pull of gravity, and the shoots grow in the opposite direction.

This way up
A miracle of nature— seedlings always come out of the soil the right way up.

Perfect poise
Keeping the center of gravity in the right place is very important—it can be embarrassing and painful if we lose our balance!

The center of gravity

Earth's gravity affects everything on the planet, living and nonliving. What is more, everything has one particular point where the effect of gravity seems to be focused. This point is known as the center of gravity. Earth's center of gravity is a point at the very center of Earth. Knowing the center of gravity is important when it comes to balancing. Think about a small child building a tower of blocks. The tower may start off neat and stable, but as little hands add brick after brick the tower becomes unstable and falls down.

The same is true of balancing in gymnastics. Gymnasts can arrange their body in a variety of positions, and as long as they keep their center of gravity relatively low and over the parts of them that are in contact with the ground, they will not fall over. But once the center of gravity falls outside their anchor points, they lose their balance and fall. The center of gravity is not just important in gymnastics. If you watch a child learning to walk, you can see how much it matters every time we move.

Overcoming Gravity

We are firmly linked to Earth. The force of gravity makes sure that however high we jump, we always come down again. The same is true for most other living things. But there are some creatures that seem to be able to defy gravity.

Flying force

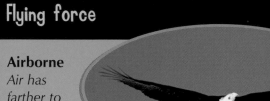

Airborne
Air has farther to travel over the top surface of a bird's wing than the lower surface, so it must travel faster.

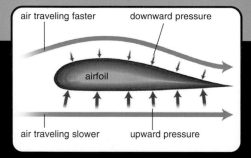

air traveling faster — downward pressure
airfoil
air traveling slower — upward pressure

A physical law, Bernoulli's Principle, says that fast-moving fluids, such as air, have lower pressure than slow-moving ones. Therefore, the upward push of the air under the wing is stronger than the downward push of the air above the wing. This means that there is an overall upward force acting on the wing.

Birds in flight

Watch birds as they fly—they swoop, glide, and dart in the air. How do they do it— can they switch off gravity? No, they cannot. But gravity acts on everything. Flying animals simply take advantage of other forces to overcome gravity.

Birds have sophisticated bodies that enable them to fly. All flying animals have to be as light as possible. Birds have hollow bones to give them the lowest possible mass. They also have big muscles to power their wings. They are streamlined to cut down on the frictional force of air resistance. But what really makes the difference is the shape of a bird's wings. They have a large surface area, and the shape of the cross-section of the wings is called an airfoil. This enables the wings to produce a lot of upward force, called lift, which acts against the weight of the bird. It is this lift that keeps the bird in the air and allows it to fly.

Aerodynamic fun

Look at the shape of a Frisbee and think about what happens to make it fly. It uses the same principles as birds and planes.

Up, up and away

In the natural world there is a limit to the size of animals that can fly. Human beings have managed to overcome those limits and design airplanes that can carry hundreds of people thousands of yards or meters up in the air. Even if you have never flown in a plane, you will have seen them flying across the sky. Have you ever wondered how so many tons of metal manage to stay up in the air?

The design of airplanes relies heavily on the same physics that makes bird flight possible. Just like birds, planes are streamlined to move through the air easily. They are kept as light as possible with the use of light, strong metals and careful design. Also like birds, planes have wings with a huge surface area and an airfoil cross-section. The engines have to be huge to accelerate the plane to a high speed. Only at very high speed does the air move fast enough across the wings to develop the lifting force needed for takeoff. A fully loaded airliner, such as a Boeing 747-400, with a full load of 400 passengers, weighs 3,969,000 newtons. Something this big needs a huge amount of lift to get it off the ground!

Who's who of flight

People have always wanted to fly, but it took a long time to find out how.

- Ancient Greece: According to an old story, Daedalus and his son, Icarus, made wings of wax and feathers. Icarus flew too close to the Sun, the wax melted, and Icarus fell to his death in the ocean.

- **1783** Joseph and Jacques Montgolfier flew the first hot-air balloon.

- **1903** Orville and Wilbur Wright made the first successful airplane flight.

- **1927** Charles Lindbergh completed the first nonstop flight across the Atlantic Ocean.

Pressure

Stand on the floor barefoot and think about how it feels. Now stand on tiptoe—the sensations will be very different. This is because by standing on your toes, you have increased the pressure on the part of your foot in contact with the floor. Pressure is a compressing, or squashing, force. It depends on both the force that is pressing and the area it is pressing on. To figure out the pressure being exerted in a particular situation, we need to know the size of the force and the area it is pressing on.

$$\text{Pressure} = \frac{\text{Force}}{\text{Area}}$$

Pressure is measured in pascals (Pa) or newtons/meter^2 (1Pa = 1N/m^2)

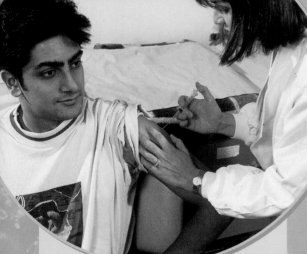

High pressure

Imagine trying to hammer a nail into a piece of wood. Everyone knows that you hit the wide end of the nail so that the pointed end goes into the wood. If you tried to do it the other way around, it would not work. Why not? The answer is pressure. With the nail the right way up, the force behind your hammer blows is all concentrated on the tiny area of the nail point. This means that intense pressure is exerted on the wood and the nail goes into it. If the wide end of the nail is next to the wood, the force of the hammer blow is spread over a much bigger area, the pressure is much lower, and the nail will not go in. Getting a shot at the doctor's office is another situation in which this principle applies.

Sharper the better
You want a very sharp needle for a shot. This is because the doctor has to apply only a tiny force to produce enough pressure to break your skin, and it is almost painless.

Monster tires

The huge tires of an industrial vehicle spread the enormous weight of the vehicle over the biggest possible area, so it does not get stuck in the mud.

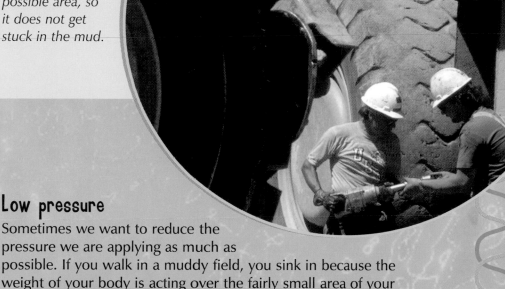

Low pressure

Sometimes we want to reduce the pressure we are applying as much as possible. If you walk in a muddy field, you sink in because the weight of your body is acting over the fairly small area of your feet. The farmers who grow our food have to drive huge vehicles in muddy fields to tend to their crops. If these vehicles sink into the mud, they can get stuck. Farmers overcome these problems by putting very wide tires onto their vehicles. These tires reduce the pressure exerted on the mud and stop them from getting stuck. Monster trucks use the same principle, and so do many off-road vehicles and even BMX bikes.

Saving lives

Sometimes understanding how pressure works can save lives. Every year during the winter, people fall through the ice on frozen ponds and rivers. Often other people fall through the ice and die trying to rescue them. A little understanding of physics can save these lives, though. Emergency services experts know that if you stand upright on the ice, your weight is pressing down on a small area. As a result the ice is likely to break. Emergency rescue teams reduce the pressure—and so the chance of the ice breaking—by lying flat on the ice. Once their weight is spread over a bigger area, they have a better chance of rescuing someone safely.

Watch Your Feet!

One quarter of all the bones in your body are found in your feet. There are about 26 bones in each foot. They are held together by a network of muscles, tendons, and ligaments. Together, all these tissues work to provide you with balance, support, and mobility. Your feet are subjected to a huge amount of force. As you run and jump, each foot may have to withstand a force of 2.5 times your body weight.

Feet and forces

For sports, you usually wear athletic shoes that are specially designed to support your feet. Some shoes, like the toeshoes worn by ballet dancers, are designed for very specific activities. But many people wear athletic shoes even when they are not planning to go for a run or work out at the gym. However, it is easy to forget that many other activities can subject our feet to just as many forces as sports. A day out shopping can involve several miles of walking, while an evening spent dancing involves exercise and foot impact just as vigorous as in any sport. Even so, the shoes we choose to wear while shopping or dancing may not be ones that will help to support our feet. Often we are more concerned about what they look like!

Looking good
People often do not consider their foot bones when choosing shoes. Yet these bones have to withstand many forces for hours at a time.

Walking with camels

Walking in soft sand is difficult, because the pressure exerted by our feet means we sink into the sand with every step. Camels manage it very well, however, because their feet are specially adapted. They are very large, and they spread out widely as the camel steps. This spreads the weight of the camel over a wide area, reducing the pressure on the sand and making sure it does not sink in.

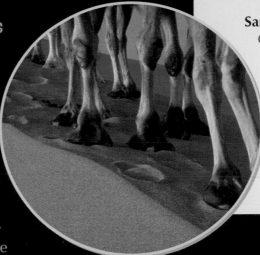

Sandy feet
Camels are much bigger and heavier than people. Yet they walk easily for miles over desert sands.

The right shoes

Why do shoes matter so much? The pressure that your feet experience will vary a lot depending on the type of shoes you are wearing. You can calculate the difference using your own feet and a couple of pairs of shoes. First calculate the force your body exerts—multiply your mass in kilograms by ten to get your weight in newtons. Then take several sheets of graph paper. Put your bare foot on one piece and draw around it, to outline the area of your foot in contact with the paper. On another piece draw around an athletic shoe. On a third piece draw around the areas of a high-heeled shoe that are in contact with the ground. You can figure out the areas of each of the tracings very roughly by counting the squares of graph paper.

Remembering that $\text{pressure} = \dfrac{\text{force}}{\text{area}}$

figure out the pressure on your foot if you stand on one leg with bare feet, wearing athletic shoes, or wearing high heels. The results can be pretty scary! Athletic shoes spread the weight of your body over a bigger area than even your bare feet, so they reduce the pressure on your foot as you exercise. But the effect of high heels is just the opposite. The bones of the feet are almost always squashed together and cramped, but the pressure exerted when someone wears heels to go dancing is potentially damaging. The result can be problems ranging from blisters to permanent deformity.

Air Pressure

We cannot see the air around us, but we certainly use it all the time as we breathe. Earth's atmosphere extends for miles above our heads. Gravity acts on all that air, pulling it downward toward Earth. Pressing down on you at sea level is an enormous force of atmospheric pressure—100,000 newtons per square meter, or the equivalent of the weight of a cow pressing down on a dinner plate! The reason we are not crushed beneath the pressure is that the fluids inside our bodies exert an equal and opposite force.

Air pressure and human health

Air pressure changes all the time. The amount of air pressing down on us also varies, depending on where we live. People living around sea level experience far greater air pressure than those who live high up on mountains—almost double in some cases. The thinner air at high altitudes contains less oxygen than air at sea level. Change in air pressure can cause real problems for people who live closer to sea level when they visit or climb mountains.

People who live high in the mountains all of their lives develop bigger lungs with a better blood supply, as well as extra red blood cells, so they have no problems with the low pressure of the air. If you move from sea level to a mountain location, you have to give your body time to make more red blood cells to help you extract enough oxygen from the air. The change often results in symptoms of altitude sickness. These symptoms can range from nausea and headaches to a loss of consciousness.

Airplanes fly high in the sky, where the air pressure is very low. This would normally be fatal for us because we would not be able to take in enough oxygen. But the cabins of airliners are pressurized, to keep us comfortable and safe.

Did you know?

When atmospheric pressure increases, gases dissolve in liquid more easily than they normally do. This is why, when you first open a container holding a fizzy drink that has been sealed under pressure, there is a rush of gases. They are coming out of solution as the pressure drops.

Finland

Norway

Sweden

United Kingdom

Denmark

Ireland

Germany

France

Italy

Spain

Air pressure and the weather

A barometer is an instrument that measures changes in air pressure, either by the movement of a column of mercury or by the changes in shape of a metal box containing air at low pressure. When the pressure is high, it supports a taller column of mercury or squashes the metal box more. Low air pressure supports less mercury or causes less squashing. These changes are transferred to a pointer on a dial showing the air pressure.

Many barometers link changes in air pressure to the weather. High air pressure, caused when air sinks and gets warmer as it is compressed, brings fine, cloudless weather. Being warmer, the air can hold more water, so clouds are less likely to form. Just the opposite happens when air at Earth's surface rises—the pressure decreases, so the air expands and cools. This is why low pressure is often associated with cloudy, wet weather.

Air pressure is also responsible for the wandering winds. Imagine blowing up a balloon—creating an area of high pressure—and then letting the air escape. Air rushes out from the high-pressure area into the rest of the room, a low-pressure area, creating a wind. This is how winds blow, from areas of high pressure to areas of low pressure. On weather maps, all areas of equal air pressure are joined together to make lines called isobars.

Forces in Fluids

Put your finger over the end of a faucet or hose while the water is running and feel the force of the water pushing against your fingers. In the same way, you can feel the pressure of water pushing down on you when you dive down into a swimming pool or the ocean. The deeper you go, the greater the weight of water pushing down on you—and water is much denser than air. Once you get down below a couple of yards or meters, you will probably start to get uncomfortable sensations in your ears. The increased pressure of the water starts to compress the air in your middle ear. This can feel really painful—you can even end up with a burst eardrum.

Water pressure under the sea

Because water is so dense, water pressure increases rapidly as you dive. While we can survive thousands of yards or meters above sea level in the reduced air pressure of high altitudes, we can go down only about 363 feet (110 m) in water before being crushed to death. What is more, gases dissolve more easily as the pressure increases. This means that as the water pressure builds up as we go deeper, nitrogen from the air in our lungs can get dissolved in the blood. If we then surface too quickly, this gas can come out of solution again very quickly in the form of bubbles in the blood. This condition, called the bends, can cause severe pain and even death. Think about what happens when you take the top off a bottle of fizzy drink and you can imagine what happens in a diver's blood. The only way people have managed to explore the really deep ocean is by traveling in submarines with specially designed hulls that can withstand the pressure without crumpling. At a depth of around 33,000 feet (10,000 m), the pressure of the water is equivalent to having a dinner plate on your head with seven elephants balanced on it!

Safe diving

If you ever go scuba diving, this is how to be sure to avoid the bends. As you return to the surface, keep your eye on the tiniest air bubbles. Make sure you follow these tiny bubbles, or go even slower. That way you will prevent the release of gas bubbles from your blood, and arrive safe at the surface.

*Objects float
when the
upthrust from the
fluid is equal to
their weight, and
that is true for
people too!*

Archimedes' principle

In the 200s BC, a Greek king
asked the inventor Archimedes
to find out if some of the gold
in his crown had been replaced
with silver, a cheaper but lighter
metal. The crown weighed and
looked as it should. Archimedes
was thinking about this as he
got into the bathtub, which
overflowed. He jumped out
of the tub and ran down the
street, shouting "Eureka!"
('I've got it!'). He had realized
he could compare the amount
of water displaced by the
crown with that displaced by
the same weight of gold. If
the gold in the crown had
been mixed with silver, it
would have a larger volume
and displace more water.
Archimedes tried this out
on the king's crown. Sure
enough, silver had been
mixed with the gold.

Floating and sinking

Imagine yourself floating in a
swimming pool, drifting with
the movements of the water.
You are buoyant—you float—
but how do you stay up? And
why, when you are in the water,
can you lift people much bigger
than yourself—people you would
not normally be able to get off the
ground? The answer is that the
force exerted by the water pushes
up on anything lowered into it.
This supporting force is known as
upthrust. Think about getting into
the bath—the water level rises
when you get in because your
body pushes some of the water
out of the way—it displaces the
water. Upthrust is equal to the
weight of fluid an object displaces.
Things feel so much lighter or
even weightless in water because
much of their weight is supported
by the upthrust.

Motion in a Curve

Many situations you encounter in physics lessons involve objects moving in straight lines. In real life, things are much more likely to move in curves than to go straight all the time. Circular motion has just as much to do with forces as any other type of movement. So what forces are acting to make things move in a curve? As we have already seen, moving objects travel in straight lines if there are no forces acting on them, or if the forces acting are balanced.

Centripetal force

Imagine yourself swinging a ball around your head on a piece of string. The momentum you give the ball in any given direction would keep it traveling in a straight line. The circular movement you see is the result of another force pulling the ball toward the center. This is centripetal force. If the centripetal force disappears—because you let go of the string—the ball will fly off in a straight line.

The level of centripetal force needed to make something move in a circle depends on several things.

Hammer-thrower
Centripetal force acting along its chain keeps this hammer moving in a circle until the athlete lets go.

- The bigger the object's mass, the bigger the centripetal force needed for circular motion. This is why small cars corner more easily than large semi trucks, and why it is easier to whirl a ball than a hammer around your head.

- The greater an object's speed, the more centripetal force is needed. A car traveling fast is more likely to leave the road on a corner. It does not have enough centripetal force to keep it going in a curve.

- The smaller the circle's radius (the tighter the curve) the greater the centripetal force needed. Accidents are more likely at tight corners than at wide bends.

Where does centripetal force come from?

When a car is turning a corner, the centripetal force it needs to stay on the road is provided by the friction between its tires and the road. The driver uses the steering wheel to change the angle of the front wheels toward the direction chosen. The centripetal force develops and turns the car. If not enough centripetal force is developed, the car cannot turn and slides off the road. The situation is made worse when roads are wet or icy. The friction between the tires and the road is reduced, so that sliding becomes more of a risk.

Cornering on a bike involves just the same sort of forces. Think back to when you were learning to ride a bike. Even when you had mastered cycling in a straight line, cornering still seemed pretty difficult. This is because to get the forces right to enable you to turn the corner, you have to lean into the corner as well as turning the handlebars. If you do not lean enough the bike will not corner, but if you lean too much the bike will topple over. Getting the centripetal force just right can be tricky!

Easy to miss
Banked tracks help competitive cyclists develop centripetal forces. Still, they do not always get it right!

Forces and Fun

Many of us have experienced the fun (or terror) of some of the huge rides at theme parks. When we take a heart-stopping loop the loop on a roller-coaster ride, we are experiencing circular motion first hand.

Forces protect you
Thanks to centripetal force, it is actually impossible for a person to fall out of the car at the top of this loop!

Fear, fun, and physics

Roller coasters and other similar rides are set up so that the centripetal force that results from the acceleration of the car and the passengers is greater than the acceleration that results from gravity when the car is at the top of the loop. Therefore, as long as the ride keeps moving at the correct speed, we cannot fall out. Theme parks allow us to experience extreme forces, and the ride designers are constantly trying to find new ways to use the forces of circular motion to give us the time of our lives. Even understanding the physics does not take away the fear—or the thrills!

Sporting spin

Anyone who is a fan of ball sports will know the importance of spinning a ball. Whether it is soccer or football, tennis or baseball, ping-pong or pool, if a player can get the ball to spin as it travels, then the possibilities for success are far greater.

To understand the importance of spin, we need to think about what happens to a ball when it is thrown normally. We launch the ball up into the air so that it travels upward and forward. It slows down as it rises, owing to both the pull of gravity and the drag effects of the frictional forces of the air. When the ball gets to the top of its flight, it begins to travel forward and downward, accelerating because of gravity, but still affected by drag forces.

Spin to win

When someone kicks the ball around the defending wall in soccer or throws a curve ball in baseball, the principle is the same. The player makes the ball spin. Depending on the direction of the spin, the relative air speed is higher on one side of the ball than on the other. This means the pressure on one side of the ball, where the air is moving fastest, is less than the pressure on the other side, where the air is moving more slowly— just like the flow of air over the wing of a bird or a plane. So there is an unbalanced force moving the ball in a curve. By varying the direction and speed of the spin they put on the ball, players can vary the amount and direction of the circular motion they set up. This makes it more difficult for opposing players to predict where the ball is going to go.

Artificial satellites

TV and telecommunications satellites depend on circular motion to keep them orbiting Earth. Once in orbit, they follow a circular path that results from centripetal forces resulting from the pull of gravity. Their speed determines their distance from Earth. Gravity will constantly pull them toward Earth's surface, but their curved path ensures that they stay in orbit.

Forces into the Future

Forces play a vital role in our lives, and in the future we will find more ways to use them and to overcome their effects.

Safer cars

One of the most risky things most of us do in our everyday lives is to travel in a car. Researchers are working on many ways to make driving safer. In every case, an understanding of forces is behind the developments.

One of the most common injuries in car accidents is whiplash. In an impact, the forces on a person's body are huge, particularly if someone runs into the back of the car in which the person is traveling. The seat pushes forward into the person's back, pushing his or her spine upright and throwing the head backward and then forward very violently. The tissues in the neck and shoulders can be very badly damaged. While the injuries are not life-threatening, they can take a very long time to heal, or leave the person with a permanent disability. However, researchers are designing new seats and headrests that mold to a person's body shape, absorbing many of the forces and supporting the head and neck far more successfully.

Safer roads

Many car accidents happen because cars skid. Intensive research is going on into possible new road surfaces to allow greater friction between cars and the road. Intelligent tire designs are also being created to increase friction when braking and cornering, but to reduce friction at high speed.

New parts for old

A lot of research has gone into developing new materials for artificial joints. For example, you have a large range of movement in your hip joint, which also has to bear all the forces as you walk, run, and jump. This joint often needs replacing as people get older. The most commonly used artificial hips have a plastic cup fitted into the joint socket in the pelvis, and a metal or ceramic head attached to the top of the femur (thigh bone). Unfortunately, most artificial hips wear out after about ten years.

Scientists are working on new materials for longer-lasting joints, such as strong ceramics that can withstand the forces applied to the joint almost as well as bone. Even more exciting, artificial bone is being developed. This will form a perfect replacement joint, and the original bone will be stimulated to grow around and into it, so eventually it will become part of the body.

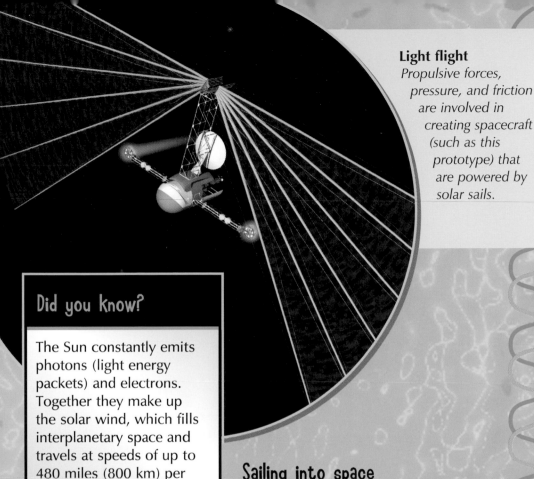

Light flight
Propulsive forces, pressure, and friction are involved in creating spacecraft (such as this prototype) that are powered by solar sails.

Did you know?

The Sun constantly emits photons (light energy packets) and electrons. Together they make up the solar wind, which fills interplanetary space and travels at speeds of up to 480 miles (800 km) per second.

Sailing into space

Space travel is limited by the time it takes us to travel anywhere and the enormous amount of fuel used. To travel farther or faster, new technology is needed to provide the propulsive forces. This is where solar sails come in.

Scientists are working to produce solar sails that will use the stream of light from the Sun to move spacecraft. A solar sail is a very thin mirror with an area of about 0.4 square mile (1 km²) made of metal-coated plastics or carbon fibers that reflect the sunlight. The idea is that each photon of light that hits the mirror exerts a tiny force on it. Because billions of photons continually strike the sail, the total force is enough to power a spacecraft. The sunlight will apply a constant pressure that will allow the spacecraft to keep accelerating because there is no drag in space. So spacecraft will eventually travel at very high speeds without needing bulky fuel. Traveling toward the stars at 54 miles (90 km) per second, a solar-sail-powered explorer could cover the distance from New York to Los Angeles in under a minute, over ten times faster than the space shuttle's orbital speed of 4.8 miles (8 km) per second.

Summary: Forces All Around Us

Forces have shaped our Earth and the universe. They have shaped life for as long as it has existed on Earth. But still, Isaac Newton and other scientists did not develop a detailed understanding of how they work until the last few centuries. This understanding of the forces in the world around us enables us to use them in many ingenious ways.

We use forces in all our methods of transportation, on land, water, through the air, or into space. We rely on the clever use of forces in sports, from events like the pole vault and the hammer throw, to the football games watched by millions. The gadgets around our home, from the can opener to the car jack, rely on forces. The industries that make everything we use depend on forces, too, for lifting and moving raw materials, parts, and finished objects.

Forces are very important in nature, for plants and animals alike. Even as you sit and read this book, bone is being dissolved from some places in your body and laid down in others, in response to the forces acting on your skeleton!

Once we know that they are there and what they do, we can find forces at work in every aspect of our lives. The existence and future of the human race depends on them!

Levers and rollers

Today's construction industry uses the same forces that the people who built Stonehenge must have used to maneuver these huge stones.

Glossary

acceleration rate of change of speed

aerodynamic designed to reduce wind drag and increase fuel efficiency

airfoil piece of material on an aircraft or other vehicle, shaped to create lift

air resistance force resisting the movement of objects through the air

airbag safety device in cars that inflates on impact

anemometer instrument for measuring wind speed

atmospheric pressure pressure exerted on Earth's surface by the gases in the atmosphere

barometer instrument for measuring air pressure

buoyant floats on fluids

cartilage firm, flexible tissue in a human or animal body that maintains shape or protects surfaces from the effects of friction

centripetal force force that pulls (acts) inward to keep objects moving in a circle

circular motion movement in a circle

compress squeeze (into less space)

crumple zones areas in the structure of a car that are designed to crumple on impact, absorbing much of the energy of a crash

curve ball in baseball, a ball that is thrown so that it curves toward or away from a batter

drag force resisting the movement of objects through a liquid or a gas

exert bring into use

femur large bone in the thigh

fluid substance that can flow, such as a gas, vapor, or liquid

force push or pull that causes a change in movement or a change in shape

friction force that affects surfaces in contact with each other, slowing down or preventing movement

fulcrum point around which a lever turns

geotropism movement of plants in response to gravity

gravity attraction between two objects that results from their mass

isobar line on a weather map connecting all the points with the same air pressure

lever simple device used to transfer force

lift upward force that acts on objects moving through the air

lubricant substance that reduces friction between two surfaces

mass amount of matter contained in a body

membrane skinlike tissue

neap tides lowest high tides in their two-week cycle

newton (N) the unit in which force is measured

newtonmeter instrument for measuring force

newtons/meter^2 (N/m^2) unit of pressure

pascals (Pa) unit of pressure; 1 Pa = 1 N/m^2

photon packet of electromagnetic radiation energy, such as light

pivot pin on which something turns or swings

pressure amount of force pressing on a given area

propulsive producing forward motion

prototype trial model for use in test runs

resistance force that delays or stops something; not conducting heat or electricity

seismograph instrument for measuring Earth tremors

solar sails new method of powering space vehicles under development

sophisticated complex, highly developed for a specific purpose

spring tides tide just after new or full Moon, when there is the greatest difference between high and low water

statolith solid body in a cell that seems to respond to gravity

stopping distance distance that a car will travel before stopping after braking at a given speed

strain gauge instrument for measuring the extent to which something changes shape

streamlined shaped to be smooth, offering the least resistance to movement through water or air

tectonic plates large areas of Earth's crust that move very slowly over Earth's surface

thrust force acting in the direction of travel

tread patterns in the material of tires that improve grip on wet roads

upthrust upward force on an object in a fluid

velocity speed

vertebrae small bones making up the spinal column

water resistance force resisting the movement of objects through water

weighbridge drive-on weighing machine for vehicles

weight force with which an object is pulled by gravity

whiplash injury to neck caused by head being jerked violently in a collision.

Further Reading

Books

Allen, Tony. *Groundbreakers: Isaac Newton*. Chicago: Heinemann Library, 2001.

Arnold, Nick. *Horrible Science: Fatal Forces*. New York: Scholastic, 1997.

The Dorling Kindersley Science Encyclopedia. New York: Dorling Kindersley, 1999.

Hunter, Rebecca. *Science, the Facts: Forces and Motion*. New York: Franklin Watts, 2003.

Parker, Steve. *Science Files: Forces*. Chicago: Heinemann Library, 2004.

Riley, Peter. *Science Topics: Forces and Motion*. Chicago: Heinemann Library, 1999.

Snedden, Robert. *Smart Science: Forces*. Chicago: Heinemann Library, 2001.

Index

acceleration 9, 16, 17, 37, 48, 49
airfoil 36, 37
airplanes 37, 42
airbags 23
air pressure 42–43
air resistance 24, 36
anemometer 12
animals and plants 6, 25, 34, 36, 41
Archimedes 45

balanced forces 14, 15, 26, 46
ball sports 49
barometer 43
Bernoulli's Principle 36
birds 25, 36
black holes 31
boat design 25
brakes 9, 17, 20
bridges 10, 12
bumpers 23
buoyancy 45

camels 41
cars 4, 9, 10, 15, 19, 20, 21, 22–23, 33, 46–47, 48, 50
cartilage 19, 33
center of gravity 35
centripetal force 46, 47, 48
circular motion 46–49
compression 11, 33, 38
cornering 46–47, 50
cranes 27
crumple zones 23
cycling 16–17, 18, 20, 21, 47

destructive forces 10
drag 16, 17, 22, 24, 49, 51

earthquakes 13

feet and shoes 40–41
force sensors 6–7
friction 16, 17, 18 21, 22, 24, 47, 49, 50
fulcrum 26, 27

geotropisms 34
gravity 4, 5, 8, 15, 28–37, 42, 48, 49
gymnastics 35

height 33

joints 19, 27, 50

levers 26–27, 52
lift 36
lifting 27
lubrication 19, 21

mass 8, 11, 17, 26, 30, 31, 36, 46
measuring forces 4, 8 9, 12–13
mechanical advantage (MA) 27
Moon 29, 30, 31, 32
movement and direction 9, 10, 18, 46
muscles 33

Newton, Sir Isaac 4, 28–29, 30
newtonmeter 8
newtons (N) 4, 8, 38

orbit 31, 49

pascals (PA) 38
penguins 25
pressure 7, 36, 38 45, 49
propulsive forces 51
pushes and pulls 4, 6, 14, 16

roller coasters 48

satellites 49
scuba diving 44
seat belts 23
seesaws 26
seismograph 13
semi trucks 10, 11
shape changes 10, 11
sharks 25
solar sails 51
solar wind 51
sound and hearing 5, 7
space travel 30, 51
speedometer 9
spin 49
steering wheels 23
stopping distances 20
strain gauges 10–11
stress 10, 11
swimming 24, 25

tectonic plates 13
thrust 16, 17, 19, 20
tides 32
tires 21, 39, 47, 50
tug of war 14

unbalanced forces 14, 15, 26, 31
upthrust 45

water pressure 44–45
water resistance 24–25
weather 43
weight 8, 10, 15, 33, 37, 39
wheelbarrows 27
whiplash 50
winds and wind power 12, 43